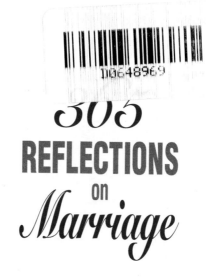

305
REFLECTIONS
on
Marriage

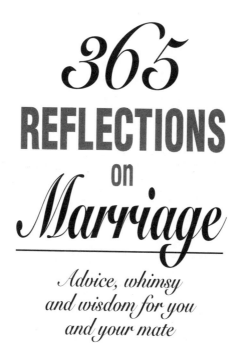

365
REFLECTIONS
on
Marriage

*Advice, whimsy
and wisdom for you
and your mate*

Eva Shaw

Adams Media Corporation
Holbrook, Massachusetts

Published by
Adams Media Corporation
260 Center Street, Holbrook, MA 02343

ISBN: 1-58062-125-2

Printed in Canada

J I H G F E D C

Library of Congress Cataloging-in-Publication Data

365 reflections on being marriage / edited by Eva Shaw.
    p. cm.
  Includes bibliographical references.
  ISBN 1-58062-125-2
  1. Marriage–Quotations, maxims, etc. I. Shaw, Eva.
II. Title: Three hundred sixty-five reflections on marriage.
PN6084.M3A145   1999
306.81–dc21   98-49353
                                          CIP

This book is available at quantity discounts for bulk purchases.
For information, call 1-800-872-5627 (in Massachusetts, 781-767-8100).

Visit our home page at http://www.adamsmedia.com

Contents

Courtship

There are times not to flirt. When you're sick. When you're with children. When you're on the witness stand.

—Joyce Jillson

I believe in love at first sight, though I don't really know if it's love.

—Barbara Hershey

I feel that the moment a date happens that it is a social encounter. And the question of sex needs to be negotiated from the first moment on.

—Camille Paglia

"Where should one use perfume?" a young woman asked. "Wherever one wants to be kissed," I said.

—Coco Chanel

Lovers behave far more respectably than married couples. Have you ever heard of a mistress-swapping party?

—Jilly Cooper

Flirtation is merely an expression of considered desire coupled with an admission of impracticability.

—Marya Mannes

The human heart, at whatever age, opens only to the heart that opens in return.

—Maria Edgeworth

If you haven't had at least a slight poetic crack in the heart, you have been cheated by nature.

—Phyllis Battelle

Then you took my hand. You told me that love was a sudden disturbance of the nerve ends that startled the fibers and made them new again.

—Barbara Guest

Do you think it is ever possible to be successful in love, if one doesn't make an effort to help things along?

—Marguerite Duras

Love is as strict as acting. If you want to love somebody, stand there and do it. If you don't, don't. There are no other choices.

—Tyne Daly

Love for the joy of loving, and not for the offerings of someone else's heart.

—Marlene Dietrich

Wherever you plan to go, plan to flirt—with the wine merchant, your butcher, the man who handles your affairs at the bank. Flirting is an honorable pastime, good for everyone's ego, and without a doubt, it slims the waistline by sending hormones zipping around your body.

—Jeanine Larmoth

Flirtatious handshakes: Finish with a tiny extra squeeze. This should not be tight, but merely a surge of energy. Then let go. Doing this signals that you are warm, confident, and something more than just pleased to meet someone—you are indicating there is a definite attraction.

—Joyce Jillson

When Shakespeare was commenting on the peculiarly bumpy road to true love, he was warning us about the stuckpoints of courtship.

—Judith Sills

The revisionist approach to romance may be difficult at first for women who thought that having your own American Express card meant never having to feign interest. But with enough practice, and enough leopard-skin scarfs, any woman should be able to act as feline as a cat. And avoid sarcasm—altogether.

—**Maureen Dowd**

If a woman asks a man on a date, she should pay for everything, including parking or taxi charges and coat check. After the first date if they want to see each other again, he should pay or they can agree to split everything. Of course, if he has money and wishes to keep paying all the time that is fine. It's an equal world, but not that equal.

—**Letitia Baldrige**

It's no use trying to sum people up. One must follow hints, not exactly what is said, not yet entirely what is done.

—**Virginia Woolf**

In nine cases out of ten, a woman had better show more affection than she feels.

—Jane Austen

Love at first sight is lust with potential—and it usually includes the potential for disaster unless the process is slowed.

—Joy Browne

Men ain't got any heart for courting a girl they can't pass—let alone catch up with.

—Jessamyn West

The mark of a true crush . . . is that you fall in love first and grope for reasons afterward.

—Shana Alexander

If it is your time love will track you down like a cruise missile. If you say, "No! I don't want it right now," that's when you'll get it for sure.

—Lynda Barry

Ever since Eve gave Adam the apple, there has been a misunderstanding between the sexes about gifts.

—Nan Robertson

Seamed stockings aren't subtle but they certainly do the job. You shouldn't wear them when out with someone you're not prepared to sleep with. . . . If you really want your escort paralytic with lust, stop frequently to adjust the seams.

—Cynthia Heimel

Love is like the measles. The older you get it, the worse the attack.

—**Mary Roberts Rinehart**

I really think that American gentlemen are the best after all, because . . . kissing your hand may make you feel very, very good, but a diamond and sapphire bracelet lasts forever.

—**Anita Loos**

I long to shout: "Mind our own business! Let us wait patiently for our counterparts. Even waiting in vain is better than willy-nilly marriage."

—**Zhang Jie**

Oh dear! How can girls like to have lovers and refuse them? I think it's dreadful.

—**Louisa May Alcott**

A lady's imagination is very rapid; it jumps
from admiration to love, from love to matrimony
in a moment.

—**Jane Austen**

The traditional male-female dynamic is enjoyable.
We like doors opened for us and meals paid for on
the first date. Otherwise we think he's cheap.

—**Christina Hoff Sommers**

A bachelor never quite gets over the idea that he is
a thing of beauty and a boy forever.

—**Helen Rowland**

When a woman looks for a husband, she usually
has a few other things in mind besides biceps and
bedrooms if she is reasonably mature.

—**Maxine Rock**

Mankind's first official attempt at dating took place in the Garden of Eden, and like most dates, it was based on a profound misunderstanding.

—**Linda Sunshine**

My boyfriend and I broke up. He wanted to get married . . . and I didn't want him to.

—**Rita Rudner**

I have noted before that there is a category of acquaintanceship that is not friendship or business or romance, but speculation, fascination.

—**Jane Smiley**

Is there anything better than to be longing for something, when you know it is within reach?

—**Greta Garbo**

On going into bars to meet first-rate men: If you want to catch trout, don't fish in a herring barrel.

—**Ann Landers**

You don't really know a person until you live with him, not just sleep with him. I staunchly believe no two people should get married until they have lived together.

—**Doris Day**

Don't compare your present lover with past ones.... Be realistic. Even with loving couples, sexual appetite waxes and wanes.

—**Dr. Ruth Westheimer**

When a date takes you out for dinner, never order chicken or spaghetti because there's no way to eat either neatly.

—**Michele Slung**

Nobody is responsible for falling in love with one person or another, but once in love, we are responsible for how we behave.

—Joy Browne

Love doesn't drop on you unexpectedly; you have to give off signals, sort like an amateur radio operator.

—Helen Gurley Brown

I don't think you can look for love. All you can do is get yourself in a situation where you don't discourage something that may be rather nice.

—Linda Ronstadt

Courtship is the process by which two people become a couple. It's an emotional process, a developmental process, that involves two essential strangers who become so close, so connected, that, at its end, they agree to live life together.

—Judith Sills

Men and women have been trying to figure out how to love each other since Adam and Eve.

—Virginia Lee

When it comes to past lovers, silence is golden and safe. If absolutely unavoidable, a quiet "so-and-so was then, you're now; the past is over, and I prefer to live the present and be with you" should suffice. Amen.

—Joy Browne

We tend to believe in love at first sight, because it combines two of the qualities we hold most dear: romance and efficiency. It's the McDonald's approach to love: instant and hot and our way.

—**Joy Browne**

We enter into relationships intent upon loving our partner to the best of our ability. We strive to understand who they are and what they need. We offer support, companionship, intimacy, and pleasure. We build them up when they're down, comfort them when they're hurting, encourage their ambitions and share their sorrow and their joy.

—**Ellen Sue Stern**

God has put into the heart of man love and the boldness to sue, and into the heart of woman fear and the courage to refuse.

—**Marguerite de Valois**

That stage of courtship which makes the most exquisite moment of youth, the freshest blossom-time of passion—when each is sure of the other's love but no formal declaration has been made, and all is mutual divination, exalting the most trivial words, the lightest gestures, into thrills delicate and delicious as wafted jasmine scent.

—**George Eliot**

In real love you want the other person's good. In romantic love you want the other person.

—**Margaret Anderson**

It is not an accident that most men start thinking of getting married as soon as they get their first job. This is not only because now they can afford it, but because having somebody at home who takes care of you is the only condition not to go crazy after a day spent on an assembly line or at a desk.

—**Silvia Federici**

If kissing and being engaged were this inflammatory, marriage must burn clear to the bone. I wondered how flesh and blood could endure the ecstasy. How did married couples manage to look so calm and unexcited.

—Jessamyn West

The best and most beautiful things in the world cannot be seen or even touched. They must be felt with the heart.

—Helen Keller

What is important to a relationship is a harmony of emotional roles and not too great a disparity in the general level of intelligence.

—Mirra Komarovsky

Trouble is a part of your life, and if you don't share it, you don't give the person who loves you enough chance to love you enough.

—**Dinah Shore**

It is better to know as little as possible of the defects of the person with whom you are to pass your life.

—**Jane Austen**

I love your lips when they're wet with wine
And red with a wicked desire.

—**Ella Wheeler Wilcox**

Marriage Proposals

When a man begins talking theoretically on the subject of children and family, pay close attention. He is sounding you out as delicately as possible.

—Judith Sills

Real marriage is the sacrificing of your ego, not for the other person, but for the relationship.

—**Oprah Winfrey**

I was at a party feeling very shy because there were a lot of celebrities around, and I was sitting in a corner alone and a very beautiful young man came up to me and offered me some salted peanuts and he said, "I wish they were emeralds," as he handed me the peanuts and that was the end of my heart. I never got it back.

—Helen Hayes

A woman won't insist on marriage. She doesn't depend on the man. In fact, she *does*, but is too brave to show it. Oh, how brave women have to be.

—Jeanne Moreau

Accept that all of us can be hurt, that all of us can—and surely will at times—fail. Other vulnerabilities, like being embarrassed or risking love, can be terrifying too. I think we should follow a simple rule: if we can take the worst, take the risk.

—Dr. Joyce Brothers

It is only by following your deepest instinct that you can lead a rich life and if you let your fear of consequence prevent you from following your deepest instinct, then your life will be safe, expedient, and thin.

—Katharine Bulter Hathaway

Faith is not making religious-sounding noises in the daytime. It is asking your inmost self questions at night—and then getting up and going to work.

—**Mary Jean Irion**

You have opened up the prison gates of my womanhood. And all the passion that was unsatisfied in me for so many years, leaped into a wild reckless storm boundless as the sea.

—**Emma Goldman**

All soft and sweet the maid appears,
With looks that know no art,
And though she yields with trembling fears,
She yields with all her heart.

—**Aphra Behn**

After a long winter
giving
each other nothing, we collide
with blossoms in our hands.

—**Fukuzoyo Chiyo**

It is very important to make sure the person you're marring is like-minded. It's crucial for a couple to have shared goals and values. The more you have in common the less you have to argue about.

—**Barbara Friedman, Director**
of Divorce and Remarriage
Counseling Center

No trumpets sound when the important decisions of our life are made. Destiny is made known silently.

—**Agnes DeMille**

And even though he insists it would take forever
to count the ways in which he loves you, let him
start counting.

—Judith Viorst

You have to understand that men can be awfully
sluggish about making decisions of the heart.
Remember, please, that evolution is a slow process.
Amphibians didn't exactly *decide* to become
reptiles. One day, one brave, scaly green guy took a
long walk on land and cautiously said, "Okay, okay,
I can handle this." That's how life science is.

—Stephanie Brush

If I lay it down as a general rule . . . that if a woman
doubts as to whether she should accept a man or
not, she certainly ought to refuse him. If she can
hesitate to "Yes," she ought to say "No," directly.

—Jane Austen

When you want something, go back and go back and go back, and don't take no for an answer. And when rejection comes, don't take it personally.

—**Betty Furness**

Marriage is a lottery in which men stake their liberty and women their happiness.

—**Virginie des Rieux**

A positive engagement to marry a certain person at a certain time, at all haps and hazards, I have always considered the most ridiculous thing on earth.

—**Jane Welsh Carlyle**

We owe it to ourselves and to our partners to bring to our marriages our best and most loving selves.

—**Sonya Rhodes**

For people willing to embrace the challenge and excitement of change, marriage can be a lifelong adventure.

—**Maxine Rock**

Brevity may be the soul of wit, but not when someone's saying "I love you." When someone's saying "I love you," he always ought to give lots of details.

—**Judith Viorst**

It is ways incomprehensible to a man that a woman should ever refuse an offer of marriage.

—**Jane Austen**

My mother said, "Marry a man with good teeth and high arches." She thought I should get that into the genetic structure of the family.

—**Jill Clayburgh**

Marriage is a social institution. It's only sensible to hesitate any time you are about to be institutionalized. If you don't have any hesitations about making a commitment, you are either (a) so ready that you're overripe, or (b) so in love that you cannot focus.

—**Judith Sills**

Knowing that destiny has brought us together . . . doesn't necessarily give us the tools to create the relationship we envision. Clarity alone isn't enough without the integrity to carry out our destiny.

—**Ellen Sue Stern**

Weddings

It might help you to be more satisfied with your mate if you remember that when you made the selection it was not multiple choice.

—**Phyllis Diller**

Talk about the joys of the unexpected; can they compare with the joys of the expected, of finding everything delightfully and completely what you knew it was going to be?

—**Elizabeth Bibesco**

It is seldom in life that one knows that a coming event is to be of crucial importance.

—**Anya Seton**

It's just time to marry, that's all . . . I'm so tired of dating! I'm so tired of keeping up a good front!

—**Anne Tyler**

A wedding is just like a funeral except you get to smell your own flowers.

—**Grace Hansen**

A good marriage is one which allows for change and growth in the individuals and in the way they express their love.

—**Pearl S. Buck**

Key axioms for women who would be wives . . .
-Keep thinking of yourself as a soft, mysterious cat.
-Always sound delighted when a man calls.
-Do not make abrupt gestures of any kind.
-If he has a girlfriend, try to become a good
 friend of hers.
-Sarcasm is dangerous. Avoid it altogether.

—**Maureen Dowd**

When the wedding march sounds the resolute approach, the clock no longer ticks, it tolls the hour. The figures in the aisle are no longer individuals, they symbolize the human race.

—Anne Morrow Lindbergh

Planning a wedding that suits everybody means sharing information—like the size of your guest list—right away.

—Judith Martin,
"Miss Manners"

Second wives have to look out for themselves more carefully than first wives because no one else is doing it for them.

—Glynnis Walker

Don't wish me happiness—I don't expect to be happy . . . it's gotten beyond that, somehow. Wish me courage and strength and a sense of humor—I will need them all.

—Anne Morrow Lindbergh

A real marriage bears no resemblance to these marriages of interest or ambition. It is two lovers who live together. A priest may well say certain words, a notary may well sign certain papers—I regard these preparations in the same way that a lover regards the rope ladder that he ties to his mistress's window.

—Lady Mary Wortley Montagu

'Tis not your saying that you love me,
Can ease me of my heart;
Your actions must your words approve,
Or else you break my heart.

—Aphra Behn

I do not expect or want you to be otherwise than you are, I love you for the good that is in you, and look for no change.

—**Mary Ann Lamb**

In the marriage union, the independence of the husband and wife will be equal, their dependence mutual, and their obligations reciprocal.

—**Lucretia Mott**

So live that when a man says he's married to you, he'll be boasting.

—**Jewish proverb**

At ceremonial events such as weddings . . . guests who are uncomfortable with one another are not supposed to show it.

—**Judith Martin,**
"Miss Manners"

The fact that one is married by no means proves that one is a mature person.

—Clara Thompson

For those who know the value and the exquisite taste of solitary freedom (for one is only free when alone), the act of leaving is the bravest and most beautiful of all.

—Isabelle Eberhardt

Wedlock: the deep, deep peace of the double bed after the hurly-burly of the chaise-longue.

—Mrs. Patrick Campbell

A girl who has a brother has a great advantage over one who hasn't; she gets a working knowledge of men without having to go through the matrimonial inquisition in order to acquire it.

—Helen Rowland

Instead of marrying "at once" it sometimes happens that we marry "at last".

—**Colette**

The people have for friends
Your common sense appall,
But the people people marry
Are the queerest folks of all.

—**Charlotte Perkins Gilman**

When two people love each other, they don't look at each other, they look in the same direction.

—**Ginger Rogers**

Everything which is exchanged between husband and wife in their life together can only be the free gift of love, can never be demanded by one or the other as a right.

—**Ellen Key**

I sometimes think the gods have united human beings by some mysterious principle, like the according notes of music. Or is it as Plato has supposed, that souls originally one have been divided, and each seeks the half it lost?

—Lydia M. Child

There is not one in a hundred of either sex who is not taken in when they marry . . . it is, of all transactions, the one in which people expect most from others, and are least honest themselves.

—Jane Austen

Most of us carry into marriage not only our childlike illusions, but we bring to it as well the demand that it *has* to be wonderful because it's *supposed* to be.

—Eda J. LeShan

The women's liberation movement has taught young females to be more careful about getting married. Many women now look very critically at a man's value system before leaping into matrimony.

—**Maxine Rock**

Most women who become second wives are blissfully unaware of what can await them on the other side of the altar.

—**Glynnis Walker**

Intimate relationships cannot substitute for a life plan. But to have any meaning or viability at all, a life plan must include intimate relationships.

—**Harriet Lerner**

Union is only possible to those who are units.
To be fit for relations in time, whether of man
or woman, one must be able to do without them in
the spirit.

—**Margaret Fuller**

People who cohabit cannot duplicate the rooting
process of marriage. They usually don't buy a
house or make other major investments as a team.
They don't often take the chance of having babies.
They don't pool paychecks or get deeply involved
in one another's parents.

—**Maxine Rock**

There is one thing I can't get in my head—
Why do people marry the people they wed?

—**Carolyn Wells**

You and your partner are forming a new family. Your wedding is the send-off party and the first joint activity of your two newly extended families. How could you expect it to be easy?

—Judith Sills

Weddings: Something women view as the perfect romantic date, as in, "Would you like to be my date for my cousin's wedding?" Men view it as the ultimate date from hell. Both views reflect the perception that it may be contagious.

—Joy Browne

The very fact that we make such a to-do over golden weddings indicates our amazement at human endurance. The celebration is more in the nature of a reward for stamina.

—Ilka Chase

With children no longer the universally accepted reason for marriage, marriages are going to have to exist on their own merits.

—**Eleanor Holmes Norton**

The sign of a good marriage is that everything is debatable and challenged; nothing is turned into law or policy. The rules, if any, are known only to the two players, who seek no public trophies.

—**Carolyn Heilbrun**

A revolutionary marriage . . . [is] one in which both partners have work at the center of their lives and must find a delicate balance that can support both together and each individually.

—**Carolyn Heilbrun**

Were marriage no more than a convenient screen for sexuality, some less cumbersome and costly protection must have been found by this time to replace it. One concludes therefore that people do not marry to cohabit; they cohabit to marry.

—Virgilia Peterson

It goes far toward reconciling me to being a woman, when I reflect that I am thus in no danger of every marrying one.

—Lady Mary Wortley Montagu

Our wedding plans pleased everybody as if we were fertilizing the earth and creating social luck.

—Marge Piercy

A wedding invitation is a beautiful and formal notification of the desire to share a solemn and joyous occasion, sent by people who have been saying, "Do we have to ask them?" to people whose first response is, "How much do you think we have to spend on them?"

—Judith Martin,
"Miss Manners"

Therefore shall a man leave his father, and his mother, and shall cleave unto his wife; and they shall be one flesh.

—Genesis 2:24

When a girl marries, she exchanges the attentions of many men for the inattention of one.

—Helen Rowland

A good marriage is at least 80 percent good luck in finding the right person at the right time. The rest is trust.

—Nanette Newman

To be happy with a man you must understand him a lot and love him a little. To be happy with a woman you must love her a lot and not try to understand her at all.

—Helen Rowland

Husbands

Sexiness wears thin after a while and beauty fades, but to be married to a man who makes you laugh every day, ah, now that's a treat.

—Joanne Woodward

Even quarrels with one's husband are preferable to the ennui of a solitary existence.

—Elizabeth Patterson
Bonaparte

If your husband wants to lick the beaters on the mixer, shut them off before you give them to him.

—Phyllis Diller

My husband and I have figured out a really good system about the housework: neither one of us does it.

—Dottie Archibald

When a man talks to you about his mother's cooking, pay no attention, for between the ages of 12 and 21, a boy can eat large quantities of anything and never feel it.

—Sarah Tyson Rorer

You see an awful lot of smart guys with dumb women, but you hardly ever see a smart woman with a dumb guy.

—Erica Jong

As a highwayman knows that he must come to the gallows at last, and acts accordingly, so a fashionably extravagant youth knows that, sooner or later, he must come to matrimony.

—Maria Edgeworth

There is so little difference between husbands you might as well keep the first.

—**Adela Rogers St. John**

Notoriously, women tolerate qualities in a lover—moodiness, selfishness, unreliability, brutality—that they would never countenance in a husband, in return for excitement, an infusion of intense feelings.

—**Susan Sontag**

Man reaches the highest point of loveableness at 12 to 17—to get it back, in the second flowering, at the age of 70 to 90.

—**Isak Dinesen**

Male and female sexuality exists like "His" and "Hers" sweaters. The measurable difference is slight but it is highly significant.

—**Beatrice Faust**

Love is not getting, but giving. It is sacrifice. And sacrifice is glorious. . . . If a man is worth loving at all, he is worth loving generously, even recklessly.

—**Marie Dressler**

A woman has got to love a bad man once or twice in her life, to be thankful for a good one.

—**Marjorie Kinnan Rawlings**

Getting along with men isn't what is important. The vital knowledge is how to get along with a man, one man.

—**Phyllis McGinley**

Trust your husband, adore your husband, and get as much as you can in your own name.

—Joan Rivers

It must be thrilling to be a man! . . . It must be consoling to know that, no matter how poor or plain or passe you may be, you can always find some woman willing to dine with you, flirt with you—and even marry you!

—Helen Rowland

So I am beginning to wonder if maybe girls wouldn't be happier if we stopped demanding so much respeckt [sic] for ourselves and developped [sic] a little more respeckt for husbands.

—Anita Loos

A wife who has sense enough to abstain from all reproaches, direct or indirect, by word or look, may reclaim her husband's affections: the bird escapes from his cage, but returns to his nest.

—**Maria Edgeworth**

⟶

My husband [Martin Luther King Jr.] often told the children that if a man had nothing that was worth dying for, then he was not fit to live.

—**Coretta Scott King**

⟶

A simple enough pleasure, sure, to have breakfast alone with one's husband, but how seldom married people in the midst of life achieve it.

—**Anne Morrow Lindbergh**

The only time a woman really succeeds in changing a man is when he's a baby.

—Natalie Wood

If one's husband dies one will not sleep.
She will lie down as if she sleeps, and if sleep overcomes her she will sleep.

But after a little while she will wake, and will not sleep. . . . When one's husband dies there is no happiness.

—Zuni Mourning Song

When two people marry, they become in the eyes of the law one person, and that one person is the husband!

—Shana Alexander

Before marriage, a man will lie awake thinking about something you said; after marriage, he'll fall asleep before you finish saying it.

—**Helen Rowland**

An archaeologist is the best husband any woman can have: the older she gets, the more interested he is in her.

—**Agatha Christie**

A supportive husband is an absolute requirement for professional women. . . .He is something she looks for, and when she finds him, she marries him.

—**Alice S. Rossi**

How to hold a man:
1. Never put makeup on at the table.
2. Never ask a man where he has been.
3. Never keep him waiting.
4. Never baby him when he is disconsolate.
5. Never fail to baby him when he is sick or has a hangover.
6. Never let him see you when you are not at your best.
7. Never talk about your other dates or boyfriends of the past.

—Mae West

I have loved many, the more and the few—
I have loved many that I might love you.

—**Grace Fallow Norton**

You asked me one day if it [marriage] seemed like giving up much for your sake. Only leave me free, as free as you are and everyone ought to be, and it is giving up nothing.

—**Antoinette Brown Blackwell**

For years [my wedding ring] has done its job. It has lead me not into temptation. It has reminded my husband numerous times at parties that it's time to go home. It has been a course of relief to a dinner companion. It has been a status symbol in the maternity ward.

—**Erma Bombeck**

As long as you give yourself and your time to a man, you can be as ambitious as you want. *Giving* is the key. The more independent you want to be, the more generous you must be with yourself as a woman.

—**Diane Von Furstenberg**

Marrying a man is like buying something you've been admiring for a long time in a show window. You may love it when you get it home, but it doesn't always go with everything else.

—**Jean Kerr**

I prefer the word "homemaker" because "housewife" always implies that there may be a wife someplace else.

—**Bella Abzug**

It is ridiculous to think you can spend your entire life with just one person. Three is about the right number. Yes, I imagine three husbands would do.

—Clare Boothe Luce

What it is that second wives really want is not more money, or fewer children, or a more secure future, it is the right to be the first priority of our husbands, the right to build lives together with them just like any other wives.

—Glynnis Walker

If the man be really the weaker vessel, and the rule is necessarily in the wife's hands, how is it then to be? To tell the truth . . . a good wife . . . keeps the glamor of love and loyalty between herself and her husband . . . the weakness never becomes apparent either to her or to him or to most lookers-on.

—Charlotte M. Yonge

This bugs me the worst. That's when the husband thinks that the wife knows where everything is, huh? Like they think the uterus is a tracking device. He comes in: "Hey Roseanne! Roseanne! Do we have any Cheetos left?" Like he can't go over and lift up the sofa cushion himself.

—**Roseanne**

The most important words in midlife are "Let Go." Let it happen to you. Let it happen to your partner. Let the feelings. Let the changes.

—**Gail Sheehy**

How to get out of admitting you're guilty even though you're guilty: Deny it. Accuse him of doing it. Tell him he drove you to it. Tell him it doesn't count because you hated it.

—**Judith Viorst**

Ah, how rewarding it is to share the bed of a really mature man. For one thing, there was the clatter and excitement four times a night as he leaped to the floor and stamped on his feet in an effort to get the circulation going. My little pet name for him, now, was Thumper.

—Jean Kerr

Women must not be blamed because they are not equal to the self-sacrifice of always meeting husbands with a smile.

—Mrs. N. F. Mossell

If a woman has her PhD in physics, has mastered quantum theory, plays flawless Chopin, was once a cheerleader, and is now married to a man who plays baseball, she will forever be "a former cheerleader married to a star athlete."

—Maryanne Ellison Simmons
(wife of Milwaukee Brewers'
catcher Ted Simmons)

The trouble with some women is that they get all excited about nothing—and then marry him.

—**Cher**

My mother said it was simple to keep a man: you must be a maid in the livingroom, a cook in the kitchen, and a whore in the bedroom. I said I'd hire the other two and take care of the bedroom bit.

—**Jerry Hall**

Whatever you may look like, marry a man your own age—as your beauty fades, so will his eyesight.

—**Phyllis Diller**

Happily
Ever
After

All my marriages were good and what follows love, or should, is deep friendship.

—**Ingrid Bergman**

That biggest blessing of loving and being loved by those I loved and respected; on earth no enjoyment certainly can be put in the balance with it.

—**Mary Rowlandson**

Every heart is the other heart. Every soul is the other soul. Every face is the other face. The individual is the one illusion.

—**Marguerite Young**

I don't need an overpowering, powerful, rich man to feel secure. I'd much rather have a man who is there for me, who really loves me, who is growing, who is real.

—Bianca Jagger

If you see the magic in a fairy tale, you can face the future.

—Danielle Steel

Making more time for sex and other pleasures goes beyond sharing chores and streamlining systems. It's a mindset, an attitude that creates a joyful awareness of ongoing opportunities for intimacy with your mate.

—Harriet Schechter

One reason we lasted so long is that we usually played two people who were very much in love. As we were realistic actors, we became those two people. So we had a divertissement: I had an affair with him, and he with me.

—Lynn Fontanne (married 55 years to costar Alfred Lunt)

Accept the pain, cherish the joys, resolve the regrets; then can come the best of benedictions— "If I had my life to live over, I'd do it all the same".

—Joan McIntosh

Love is moral even without legal marriage, but marriage is immoral without love.

—Ellen Key

Happiness is a sort of atmosphere you can live in sometimes when you're lucky. Joy is a light that fills you with hope and faith and love.

—**Adela Rogers St. John**

Love vanquishes time. To lovers, a moment can be eternity, eternity can be the tick of a clock.

—**Mary Parrish**

Marriage is tough, because it is woven of all these various elements, the weak and the strong.

—**Anne Morrow Lindbergh**

I think women need kindness more than love. When one human being is kind to another, it's a very deep matter.

—**Alice Childress**

Set aside a few moments to clear your mind and, if you've had a disagreement with your mate, to clear the air. Count your blessings together and tell each other all the things you love about each other.

—**Harriet Schechter**

There's a period of life when we swallow a knowledge of ourselves and it becomes either good or sour inside.

—**Pearl Bailey**

Do not rely completely on any other human being, however dear. We meet all life's greatest tests alone.

—**Agnes Macphail**

Be willing to shed parts of your previous life. For example, in our 20s we wear a mask; we pretend to know more than we do. We must be willing, as we get older, to shed cocktail party phoniness and admit, "I am who I am".

—**Gail Sheehy**

Once you can laugh at your own weaknesses, you can move forward. . . . It opens people up. If you're good, you can fill up those openings with something positive. Maybe you can combat some of the ugliness in the world.

—**Goldie Hawn**

Beware of allowing a tactless word, a rebuttal, a rejection to obliterate the whole sky.

—**Anaïs Nin**

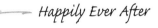

Learn by practice. Whether it means to learn to dance by practicing dancing or to live by practicing living, the principles are the same.

—**Martha Graham**

Say "I love you" to those you love. The eternal silence is long enough to be silent in, and that awaits us all.

—**George Eliot**

We all need somebody to talk to. It would be good if we talked to each other—not just pitter-patter, but real talk. . . . It's so much easier to be together when we drop our masks.

—**Liv Ullmann**

The way I see it, if you want the rainbow, you gotta put up with the rain.

—**Dolly Parton**

Asking your mother-in-law to respect your privacy is fine — as long as the request is delivered by your husband.

—Judith Martin,
"Miss Manners"

If evolution, as applied to sex, teaches any one lesson plainer than another, it is the lesson that the monogamic marriage is the basis of all progress.

—Antoinette Brown Blackwell

Marriage is a business of taking care of a man and rearing his children . . . it ain't meant to be no perpetual honeymoon.

—Clare Boothe Luce

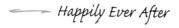

I have always detested the belief that sex is the chief bond between man and woman. Friendship is far more human.

—**Agnes Smedley**

You mustn't force sex to do the work of love or love to do the work of sex—that's quite a thought, isn't it.

—**Mary McCarthy**

Lust is what makes you keep wanting it, even when you have no desire to be with each other. Love is what makes you keep wanting to be with each other, even when you have no desire to do it.

—**Judith Viorst**

Almost all married people fight, although many are ashamed to admit it. Actually, a marriage in which no quarreling takes place may well be one that is dead or dying from emotional undernourishment. If you care, you probably fight.

—**Flora Davis**

After a certain age, if one lives in the world, one can't be astonished—that's a lost pleasure.

—**Maria Edgeworth**

Let no one ever say that marriages are made in heaven; the gods would not commit so great an injustice!

—**Marguerite de Valois**

Put off your shame with your clothes when you go in to your husband, and put it on again when you come out.

—**Theano**

If you don't endeavor that there be not a better husband and wife in the world than yourselves, you will always be wishing for that which you shall think best.

—**Aspasia**

By now I know the things I know.
And do the things I do,
And if you do not like me so,
To hell, my love, with you.

—**Dorothy Parker**

Dawn love is silver
Wait for the west:
Old love is gold love
Old is the best.

—**Katherine Lee Bates**

What we must learn, above all, is that if ever there is a time for the "marriage glass" to be filled to the brim, mid-life is that time.

—**Sonya Rhodes**

So each will have two lives, a doubled state;
Each in himself will live, and in his mate.

—**Louise Labé**

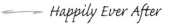

Sometimes idiosyncrasies which used to be irritating become endearing, part of the complexity of a partner who has become woven deep into our own selves.

—**Madeleine L'Engle**

At mid-life, couples are striving for great intimacy and maximum independence in their marriages. It's a fine balance to strike—getting closer and giving each other space at the same time.

—**Sonya Rhodes**

"In love" is fragile for it is woven only with the gossamer threads of beauty. It seems to be absurd to talk about "happy" and "unhappy" marriages.

—**Anne Morrow Lindbergh**

While we don't have the power to change our partner, we *do* have the power to change our approach. We can start to do this by looking at the gap between our expectations and reality.

—**Ellen Sue Stern**

A long-term marriage has to move beyond chemistry to compatibility, to friendship, to companionship. It is certainly not that passion disappears, but that it is conjoined with other ways of love.

—**Madeleine L'Engle**

Nothing in life is as good as the marriage of true minds between man and woman. As good? It is life itself.

—**Pearl S. Buck**

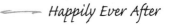

There is nothing more lovely in life than the union of two people whose love for one another has grown through the years from the small acorn of passion to a great rooted tree.

—**Vita Sackville-West**

In a successful marriage, there is no such thing as one's way. There is only the way of both, only the bumpy, dusty, difficult, but always mutual path!

—**Phyllis McGinley**

Marriage is not just spiritual communion and passionate embraces; marriage is also three meals a day, sharing the workload and remembering to carry out the trash.

—**Dr. Joyce Brothers**

In love there are no vacations; no such thing. Love has to be lived fully with its boredom and all that.

—**Marguerite Duras**

I know some good marriages—marriages where both people are just trying to get through their days by helping each other, being good to each other.

—**Erica Jong**

Marriage always demands the greatest understanding of the art of insincerity possible between two human beings.

—**Vicki Baum**

One advantage of marriage, it seems to me, is that when you fall out of love with him, or he falls out of love with you, it keeps you together until you maybe fall in love again.

—**Judith Viorst**

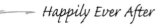

After a few years of marriage a man can look right at a woman without seeing her and a woman can see right through a man without looking at him.

—**Helen Rowland**

It takes a long time to be really married. One marries many times at many levels within a marriage. If you have more marriages than you have divorces within the marriage, you're lucky and you stick it out.

—**Ruby Dee**

The long-term accommodation that protects marriage and other such relationships is . . . forgetfulness.

—**Alice Walker**

Families

The thing that impresses me the most about America is the way parents obey their children.

—**King Edward VIII**

Here is the beginning of understanding: most parents are doing their best, and most children are doing their best, and they're doing pretty well, all things considered.

—**Richard Louv**

Parenting is not logical. If it were, we would never have to read a book, never need a family therapist, and never feel the urge to call a close friend late at night for support after a particularly trying bedtime scene. . . . We have moments of logic, but life is run by a much larger force. Life is filled with disagreement, opposition, illusion, irrational thinking, miracle, meaning, surprise, and wonder.

—**Jeanne Elium and Don Elium**

It is not a bad thing that children should occasionally, and politely, put parents in their place.

—**Colette**

Parents learn a lot from their children about coping with life.

—**Muriel Spark**

The family is like a book: the children are the leaves, the parents are the covers that protective beauty gives. At first the pages of the book are blank and purely fair, but time soon writeth memories and painteth pictures there. Love is the little golden clasp that bindeth up the trust; Oh, break it not, lest all the leaves shall scatter and be lost.

—**Anonymous**

Home is the place where, when you have to go there, they have to take you in.

—**Robert Frost**

Family values are a little like family vacations — subject to changeable weather and remembered more fondly with the passage of time. Though it rained all week at the beach, it's often the momentary rainbows that we remember.

—**Leslie Dryfous**

Families name us and define us, give us strength to embrace or escape their influence. They are magnets that both hold us close and drive us away.

—**George Howe Colt**

Soup is a lot like a family. Each ingredient enhances the others; each batch has its own characteristics; and it needs time to simmer to reach full flavor.

—**Marge Kennedy**

[Family] bonds are formed less by moments of celebration and of crisis than by the quiet, undramatic accretion of minutiae — the remark on the way out the door, the chore undone, the unexpected smile.

—**George Howe Colt**

Call it a clan, call it a network, call it a tribe, call it a family. Whatever you call it, whoever you are, you need one.

—**Jane Howard**

The family — that dear octopus from whose tentacles we never quite escape, nor, in our inmost hearts, ever quite wish to.

—**Dodie Smith**

If the family were a fruit, it would be an orange, a circle of sections, held together but separable — each segment distinct.

—**Letty Cottin Pogrebin**

We are born into them, marry into them, even create them among the people we love. They come large and extended . . . or small and nuclear. But whatever their size or wherever they live, strong families give us the nurturance and strength we need in order to survive.

—**Andrea Davis**

Families are the most beautiful things in all the world.

—**Louisa May Alcott**

A mother's love for her child is like nothing else in the world. It knows no law, no pity, it dares all things and crushes down remorselessly all that stands in its pass.

—**Agatha Christie**

No one had told her what it would be like, the way she loved her children. What a thing of the body it was, as physically rooted as sexual desire, but without its edge of danger.

—**Mary Gordon**

A mother . . . is forever surprised and and even faintly wronged that her sons and daughters are just people, for many mothers hope and half expect that their newborn child will make the world better, will somehow be a redeemer. Perhaps they are right, and they can believe that the rare quality they glimpsed in the child is active in the unburdened adult.

—Florida Scott-Maxwell

Loving a child doesn't mean giving in to all his whims; to love him is to bring out the best in him, to teach him to love what is difficult.

—Nadia Boulanger

Motherhood has been the most joyous and important experience in my life. I would die for my children.

—Carly Simon

To talk to a child, to fascinate him, is much more difficult than to win an electoral victory. But it is more rewarding.

—**Colette**

Even though fathers, grandparents, siblings, memories of ancestors are important agents of socialization, our society focuses on the attributes and characteristics of mothers and teachers and gives them the ultimate responsibility for the child's life chances.

—**Sara Lawrence Lightfoot**

You might not have thought it possible to give birth to others before one has given birth to oneself, but I assure you it is quite possible, it has been done; I offer myself in evidence as Exhibit A.

—**Sheila Ballantyne**

With two sons born eighteen months apart, I operated mainly on automatic pilot through the ceaseless activity of their early childhood. I remember opening the refrigerator late one night and finding a roll of aluminum foil next to a pair of small red tennies. Certain that I was responsible for the refrigerated shoes, I quickly closed the door and ran upstairs to make sure I had put the babies in their cribs instead of the linen closet.

—**Mary Kay Blakely**

The frequency of personal questions grows in direct proportion to your increasing girth. . . . No one would ask a man such a personally invasive question as "Is your wife having a natural childbirth or is she planning to be knocked out?" But someone might ask that of you. No matter how much you wish for privacy, your pregnancy is a public event to which everyone feels invited.

—**Jean Marzollo**

I remember leaving the hospital . . . thinking, "Wait, are they going to let me just walk off with him? I don't know beans about babies! I don't have a license to do this. [We're] just amateurs."

—Anne Tyler

Life is crazy. Now, maybe you knew this all along. But before I had children, I actually held on to the illusion that there was some sense of order in the universe. . . . I am now convinced that we are all living in a Chagall painting — a world where brides and grooms and cows and chickens and angels and sneakers are all mixed up together, sometimes floating in the air, sometimes upside down and everywhere.

—Susan Lapinski

Making the decision to have a child — it's momentous. It is to decide forever to have your heart go walking around outside your body.

—Elizabeth Stone

Five years ago I thought the most courageous thing was not to get married, not to have children. That all seemed so predictable and safe. Now I think the most courageous thing is to get married and *have* children, because that seems the most worthwhile.

—**Candice Bergen**

I used to be a reasonably careless and adventurous person before I had children; now I am morbidly obsessed by seat belts and constantly afraid that low-flying aircraft will drop on my children's school.

—**Margaret Drabble**

Truth, which is important to a scholar, has got to be concrete. And there is nothing more concrete than dealing with babies, burps and bottles, frogs and mud.

—**Jeanne J. Kirkpatrick**

One of the things I've discovered in general about raising kids is that they really don't give a damn if you walked five miles to school. They deal with what's happening now.

—**Patty Duke**

He opened the jar of pickles when no one else could. He was the only one in the house who wasn't afraid to go into the basement by himself. He cut himself shaving, but no one kissed it or got excited about it. It was understood that when it rained, he got the car and brought it around to the door. When anyone was sick, he went out to get the prescription filled. He took lots of pictures . . . but he was never in them.

—**Erma Bombeck**

To this day I cannot see a bright daffodil, a proud gladiola, or a smooth eggplant without thinking of Papa. Like his plants and trees, I grew up as part of his garden.

—**Leo Buscaglia**

Govern a small family as you would cook a small fish, gently.

—**Chinese proverb**

One night at about two o'clock in the morning, my father caught a man stealing bananas from our backyard. He went over to the man with his machete, took the bananas, cut the bunch in half and said, "Here, you can have it." And then he said, "From now on, if you need anything from the back of our house, come to the front."

—**Chi Chi Rodriguez**

My father was as compulsive and efficient as I am. At Saturday morning breakfast, he would give each of us a list of chores that we had to get done for the day before any free time. My mother would get very upset when she got a list.

—**David Fissel**

Father was never late. Indeed, punctuality was his eleventh commandment. He saw lateness as a signal to the boss that you didn't care about your job, a potentially suicidal misstep. "If you're to be there at seven," he lectured me, "you be there at six forty-five. And you don't go to the water bucket more than once an hour."

—**Dan Rather**

I know fame and power are for the birds. But then suddenly life comes into focus for me. And, ah, there stand my kids. I love them.

—**Lee Iacocca**

A man finds out what is meant by a spitting image when he tries to feed cereal to his infant.

—**Imogene Fay**

The debt of gratitude we owe our mother and father goes forward, not backward. What we owe our parents is the bill presented to us by our children.

—**Nancy Friday**

The roaring of the wind is my wife and the stars through the window pane are my children.

—**John Keats**

The most important thing a father can do for his children is to love their mother.

—**Theodore Hesburgh**

Not only do our wives need our support, but our children need our deep involvement in their lives. If this period [the early years] of primitive needs and primitive caretaking passes without us, it is lost forever. We can be involved in other ways, but never again on this profoundly intimate level.

—Augustus Y. Napier

The first handshake in life is the greatest of all: the clasp of an infant's fist around a parent's finger.

—Mark Beltaire

Allow children to be happy in their own way, for what better way will they ever find?

—Samuel Johnson

Don't demand respect, as a parent. Demand civility and insist on honesty. But respect is something you must earn — with kids as well as adults.

—William Attwood

The best brought up children are those who have seen their parents as they are. Hypocrisy is not the parents' first duty.

—George Bernard Shaw

Parents lend children their experience and a vicarious memory; children endow their parents with a vicarious immortality.

—George Santayana

Romance fails us and so do friendships, but the relationship of parent and child, less noisy than all others, remains indelible and indestructible, the strongest relationship on earth.

—**Theodore Reik**

When you have children, you begin to understand what you owe your parents.

—**Japanese Proverb**

Children have never been very good at listening to their elders, but they have never failed to imitate them.

—**James Baldwin**

Even if society dictates that men and women should behave in certain ways, it is fathers and mothers who teach those ways to children — not just in the words they say, but in the lives they lead.

—Augustus Y. Napier

Children are natural mimics — they act like their fathers or mothers in spite of every attempt to teach them good manners.

—Anonymous

What children expect from grownups is not to be "understood," but only to be loved, even though this love may be expressed clumsily or in sternness. Intimacy does not exist between generations — only trust.

—Carl Zucker

An atmosphere of trust, love, and humor can nourish extraordinary human capacity. One key is authenticity; parents acting as people, not as roles.

—**Marilyn Ferguson**

To raise good human beings it is not only necessary to be a good mother and a good father, but to have had a good mother and father.

—**Marcelene Cox**

Three stages in a parent's life: nutrition, dentition, tuition.

—**Marcelene Cox**

Anything which parents have not learned from experience they can now learn from their children.

—Anonymous

Always end the name of your child with a vowel, so that when you yell, the name will carry.

—Bill Cosby

It will help us and our children if we can laugh at our faults. It will help us tolerate our shortcomings and it will help our children see that the goal is to be human, not perfect.

—Neil Kurshan

Give a little love to a child, and you will get a great deal back.

—**John Ruskin**

Let children know you are human. It's important for children to see that parents are human and make mistakes. When you're sorry about something you've said or done, apologize! It is best when parents apologize in a manner that is straightforward and sincere.

—**Saf Lerman**

Wit,
Wisdom,
and Advice

Let me tell you, a discussion that starts, "I'll tell you something you do that irritates me, if you tell me something I do that bothers you," never ends in a hug and a kiss.

—**Phyllis Diller**

There is only one sex. . . . A man and a woman are so entirely the same thing that one can scarcely understand the subtle reasons for sex distinction with which our minds are filled.

—**George Sand**

Sex is a serious undertaking. My view is more spiritual. It's the most intimate exchange of human energy. You live with the interaction of those sparks for a long time afterwards.

—**Shirley MacLaine**

I'd lots of affairs before I married, just love affairs, not sex-love affairs. We'd neck and hug and kiss and play with each other. But no sex. Not 'til I got married. Probably one of the reasons I did get married. . . . I was 17.

—Mae West

Women have served all these centuries as looking glasses possessing the magic and delicious power of reflecting the figure of man at twice its natural size.

—Virginia Woolf

Toleration . . . is the greatest gift of the mind; it requires the same effort of the brain that it takes to balance oneself on a bicycle.

—Helen Keller

Some men break your heart in two,
Some men fawn and flatter,
Some men never look at you,
and that cleans up the matter.

—**Dorothy Parker**

I love being married. It's so great to find one special person you want to annoy for the rest of your life.

—**Rita Rudner**

One doesn't have to get anywhere in a marriage. It's not a public conveyance.

—**Iris Murdoch**

Marriage . . . is one of the events in our society that marks you as an adult. Yes, you can be an adult without being married. And yes, plenty of people marry without having done much growing up.

—Judith Sills

A woman isn't complete without a man. But where do you find a man—a real man—these days?

—Lauren Bacall

Only really plain people know about love—the very fascinating ones try so hard to create an impression that they soon exhaust their talents.

—Katharine Hepburn

It's hard when you don't like someone a friend marries. . . . [I]t means that even a simple flat inquiry like, "How's Helen?" is taken amiss, since your friend always thinks what you hope he's going to say is "Dead."

—Nora Ephron

Most people come into a relationship with hopes and dreams and plans for the future. They also bring with them, however, all their stuff, not to mention years and years worth of habits and attitudes. Trying to blend all this stuff . . . can be a nightmare.

—Harriet Schechter

Be on the alert to recognize your prime at whatever time of your life it may occur.

—Muriel Spark

The morality I learned at home required marriage. I just couldn't have an affair. So I got married all those times and now I'm accused of being a scarlet woman.

—Elizabeth Taylor

If you're looking for the perfect way to kill romance and intimacy, put an office in your bedroom and keep it cluttered with visible reminders of all the work that awaits you there.

—Harriet Schechter

Until you make peace with who you are, you'll never be content with what you have.

—Doris Mortman

Some people are more turned on by money than they are by love. . . . In one respect they're alike. They're both wonderful as long as they last.

—**Abigail Van Buren**

Women complain about sex more often than men. Their gripes fall into two major categories: (1) Not enough. (2) Too much.

—**Ann Landers**

Just don't give up trying to do what you really want to do. Where there's love and inspiration, I don't think you can go wrong.

—**Ella Fitzgerald**

The trick is not how much pain you feel but how much joy you feel. Any idiot can feel pain. Life is full of excuses to feel pain, excuses not to live, excuses, excuses, excuses.

—**Erica Jong**

Take time to say "I love you" at least daily to each other. Even though actions often speak louder than words, words are important, too.

—**Harriet Schechter**

When we do the best we can, we never know what miracle is wrought in our life, or in the life of another.

—**Helen Keller**

Keep a green tree in your heart and perhaps the singing bird will come.

—**Chinese proverb**

If you believe, then you hang on. If you believe, it means you've got imagination, you don't need stuff thrown out for you in a blueprint, you don't face facts—what can stop you?

—Ruth Gordon

Marriage accustomed one to the good things, so one came to take them for granted, but it magnified the bad things, so they came to feel as painful as a grain in one's eye.

—Marilyn French

Men are like the earth and we are the moon; we turn always one side to them, and they think there is no other, because they don't see it—but there is.

—Olive Schreiner

Beware of fainting fits . . . though at the time they may be refreshing and agreeable yet believe me they will in the end, if too often repeated and at improper seasons, prove destructive to your constitution.

—**Jane Austen**

There are only two things that are absolute realities, love and knowledge, and you can't escape them.

—**Olive Schreiner**

It ever has been since time began
And ever will be, till time lose breath,
That love is a mood—no more—to man
And love to a women is life or death.

—**Ella Wheeler Wilcox**

The sexes in each species of beings . . . are always true equivalents—equals but not identicals.

—**Antoinette Brown Blackwell**

Most women would rather have someone whisper their name at optimum moments than rocket with contractions to the moon.

—**Merle Shain**

Face your deficiencies and acknowledge them; but do not let them master you. Let them teach you patience, sweetness, insight.

—**Helen Keller**

Love doesn't just sit there, like a stone, it has to be made, like bread; re-made all the time, made new.

—**Ursula K. Le Guin**

All married couples should learn the art of battle as they should learn the art of making love. Good battle is objective and honest—never vicious and cruel. Good battle is healthy and constructive, and brings to the marriage the principle of equal partnership.

—Ann Landers

You gain strength, courage, and confidence by every experience in which you really stop to look fear in the face.

—Eleanor Roosevelt

When all is said and done, monotony may after all be the best condition for creation.

—Margaret Sackville

We all go through the same things—it's all just a different kind of same thing.

—**Susan Glaspell**

We cooked, cleaned, labored, worried, planned, we wept and laughed, we groaned and we sang, but we never despaired.

—**Kathleen Norris**

Marriage is the only thing that affords a woman the pleasure of company and the perfect sensation of solitude at the same time.

—**Helen Rowland**

Life is a patchwork—here and there,
Scraps of pleasure and despair
Join together, hit or miss.

—**Anne Bronaugh**

I have no patience with women who measure and weigh their love like a country doctor dispensing capsules.

—**Marie Dressler**

A man who marries a showy entertaining coquette, and expects she will make him a charming companion for life, commits as absurd a blunder as that of the famous nobleman who, delighted with the wit and humor of Punch at a puppet-show, bought Punch, and ordered him to be sent home for his private amusement.

—**Maria Edgeworth**

For when a man is in love's grip
it's wrong for him to knowingly
ignore his lady's orders.

—**Domna H. (12th century)**

Jealousy has always been the whetstone of love
and some would say that without it love does not
have its inner shiver.

—Edna O'Brien

Life can be wildly tragic at times, and I've had my
share. But whatever happens to you, you have to
keep a slightly comic attitude. In the final analysis,
you have got not to forget to laugh.

—Katharine Hepburn

Always leave home with a tender good-bye and
loving words. They may be the last.

—*Hill's Manual of Social and
Business Forms*, 1887

We fluctuate long between love and hatred before
we can arrive at tranquility.

—Heloise (c. 1098–1164)

The only marriage with partners strong enough to risk divorce is strong enough to avoid it.

—**Carolyn Heilbrun**

Little drops of water, little grains of sand
Every sensible woman got a back-door man.

—**Sara Martin**

When there are children and bank accounts in common, both partners have more inducement to work out problems and stay married.

—**Maxine Rock**

Lust is fun and has its place both in courtship and in marriage, but it is only one component of mate selection.

—**Maxine Rock**

The North American marriage idea is one of the most conspicuous examples of our insistence on hitching our wagons to a star. It is one of the most difficult marriage forms that the human race has ever attempted.

—**Margaret Mead**

Your basic extended family today includes your ex-husband or -wife, your ex's new mate, your new mate, possibly your new mate's ex, and any new mate that your new mate's ex has acquired.

—**Delia Ephron**

We all have our own idea of what marriage is, but when you break it down to its most basic components, it is a union between two people who care about each other enough to want to make a life together.

—**Glynnis Walker**

Anyone must see at a glance that if men and women marry those who they do not love, they must love those whom they do not marry.

—**Harriet Martineau**

The spirit of the marriage left the bedroom and took to living in the parlor.

—**Zora Neale Hurston**

In great romance, each person basically plays a part that the other really likes.

—**Elizabeth Ashley**

Love and life cannot help but marry and stay married with an exhausting violence of fidelity.

—**Kate O'Brien**

Being married was like having a hippopotamus sitting on my face. . . . Hippopotamuses aren't all bad. They are what they are. But I wasn't meant to have one sitting on my face.

—**Faith Sullivan**

I cannot abide the Mr. and Mrs. Noah attitude toward marriage; the animals went in two by two, forever stuck together with glue.

—**Vita Sackville-West**

I know a lot of wonderful men married to pills, and I know a lot of pills married to wonderful women. So one shouldn't judge that way.

—**Barbara Bush**

Keep the other person's well-being in mind when you feel an attack of soul-purging truth coming on.

—**Betty White**

If the husband and wife can possibly afford it, they should definitely have separate bathrooms for the sake of their marriage.

—**Doris Day**

We get trapped into intellectually debating who's right and who's wrong and there's only so far we can go. Taking his hand or embracing him at the right moment can be a miraculous healing agent, beyond what words can say.

—**Ellen Sue Stern**

It is very difficult to live among people you love and hold back from offering them advice.

—**Anne Tyler**

Chains do not hold a marriage together. It is threads, hundreds of tiny threads, which sew people together through the years.

—**Simone Signoret**

It seems to me that the desire to get married—which, I regret to say, I believe is basic and primal in women—is followed almost immediately by an equally basic and primal urge—which is to be single again.

—**Nora Ephron**

Some pray to marry the man they love
My prayer will somewhat vary:
I humbly pray to heaven above
That I love the man I marry.

—**Rose Pastor Stoke**

Bibliography

Andrews, Robert. *The Concise Columbia Dictionary of Quotations*, New York: Columbia University Press, 1989.

Barreca, Regina. *The Penguin Book of Women's Humor*, New York: Penguin Books: 1996.

Biggs, Mary. *The Columbia Book of Quotations by Women*, New York: Columbia University Press, 1996.

Brown, Joy. *Why They Don't Call When They Say They Will and Other Mixed Signals*, New York: Simon and Schuster, 1989.

Crawley, Tony. *Chambers Film Quotes*, New York: Chambers, 1991.

Douglas, Charles Noel. *Forty Thousand Quotations Prose and Poetical*, Garden City, NJ: Halcyon House, 1940.

Evans, Bergen. *Dictionary of Quotations*: New York; Avenel Books, 1968.

Flesch, Rudolf. *The New Book of Unusual Quotations*, New York: Harper and Row, 1966.

Lee, Virginia. *Affairs of the Heart*, Freedom, CA: Crossing Press, 1993.

Linfield, Jordan L. and Joseph Krevisky. *Words of Love*, New York: Random House, 1997.

Maggio, Rosalie. ed. *The Beacon Book of Quotations by Women*, Boston: Beacon Press, 1992.

Partnow, Elaine. *The New Quotable Woman*, New York: Meridian Press, 1993.

The Quotable Woman, Philadelphia: Running Press, 1991.

Rhodes, Sonya. *The Second Honeymoon*, New York: William Morrow, 1992.

Riley, Dorothy Winbush. *My Soul Looks Back, 'les I Forget: A Collection of Quotations by People of Color*. New York: HarperCollins, 1991.

Rock, Maxine. *The Marriage Trap*, Atlanta: PeachTree Publishers, 1986

Safire, William and Leonard Safir. *Words of Wisdom*, New York: Fireside Book, 1989.

Schechter, Harriet and Vicki T. Gibbs. *More Time for Sex*, New York: Penguin, 1996.

Sherrin, Ned. *The Oxford Dictionary of Humorous Quotations*, New York: Oxford University Press, 1996.

Sills, Judith, Ph.D. *A Fine Romance*, Los Angeles: Jeremy P. Tarcher, Inc., 1987.

Simpson, James B., ed. *Simpson's Contemporary Quotations*, Boston: Houghton Mifflin, 1988.

Stern, Ellen Sue. *Loving an Imperfect Man*, New York: Pocket Books, 1997.

Walker, Glynnis. *Second Wife, Second Best?*, New York: Doubleday 1984.